How to Hire Quality Employees On The Planet Earth | The Ul
Employer's Guide To Not Being Held Hostage
ISBN 979-8-9864278-5-0
Copyright © 2018 by Clay Clark

Clay Clark Publishing

Published by Clay Clark Publishing
3920 W 91st Street South
Tulsa, Ok 74132

Clay Clark Publishing books may be purchased for educational, business or sales promotional use. For more information, please email the Special Markets Department at info@ThriveTimeShow. com. For a good time visit ThriveTimeShow.com

TABLE OF CONTENTS

A QUICK HARD LOOK AT T ABOUT AMERI EMPLO

STATISTICAL

HE TRUTH

A'S CURRENT

OYEES:

h is just knowing the facts.

As of the time that I am writing this book, the unemployment rate in America stands at a rate that is hovering between 3.75% to 4%, yet according to **the U.S. Chamber and CBS News,** "75% of employees are stealing from the workplace," (CBS News - Employee Theft: Are You Blind to It?) **according to Inc. Magazine,** "85% of employers caught applicants fibbing on their résumés or applications," (Inc. Magazine - 85 Percent of Job Applicants Lie on Resumes. Here's How to Spot a Dishonest Candidate) **and according to the Washington Post** "78% of the men that you are interviewing admit to having cheated on their partner (spouse)" (Washington Post - Five Myths About Cheating.) **Why is this important to know? It's because it's important** for you to know that the vast majority of people (at least 85% of people) are not behaving like good people. Most people are not good people. And before reading this chapter, I believe that deep down you want to believe that most people are "honest, decent and hard-working Americans who are trying to do the best that they can to earn a living and to provide for their families," just like I once did. However, this belief is only true if you are running a business that only employs the honest and hard working 15% of the population, which I have actually thought about doing. My friend, most employees are going to come to work with you because they are excited about a new "opportunity" for growth and then they are going to go through the following predictable cycle by default that I call, "spoiling on their expiration date."

STEP 1

THE "DATING" PHASE

They are going to dress up everyday for their new job like they are going on a first date.

During the interview process and when Kermit showed up to work for his first day of work he dressed to impress. Oh, yes, he did dress to impress, and do you want to know why? He dressed to impress because he wanted you to believe that he was a nice-dressing, high-quality and dependable employee you could trust. In fact, subconsciously, I believe that at this point in the hiring process, Kermit actually believed that this was finally going to be the job where he would gain traction because he had decided that he was not going to screw things up this time. He believed he was actually going to try hard at this job because here he could make a career. And for those first few euphoric weeks of employment, Kermit honors the promises that he made to himself and to you. In fact, at first, Kermit not only showed up to work on time, but he actually showed up early to show you that he was serious about his career. And although Kermit knew that you were busy managing the other 50 + responsibilities and employees that you were responsible for every day, he's just "slightly frustrated that you didn't even recognize him for arriving early to work three days in a row."

FUN FACT

"*85 Percent of Job Applicants Lie on Résumés.*"

- Inc.com

85 Percent of Job Applicants Lie on Résumés.
Here's How to Spot a Dishonest Candidate

STEP 2

THE "EXCUSE" PHASE

Dressing Up Less and Showing Up to Work Late...

On Occasion.

After 41 days on the job, and over time you begin to notice Kermit dressing up less and less and actually beginning to show up to work wearing clothing that is slightly out of dress code, while being 1 to 2 minutes late for every meeting. After working diligently for you THREE INCREDIBLE WEEKS IN A ROW, Kermit is growing frustrated with you, and the job because you have yet to recognize him for his potential to be the best employee you've ever had and you haven't yet promoted him to super levels of management based on his first three weeks with you. So, on a Thursday night, Kermit subconsciously wants to teach you a lesson when he agreed to go out with his friends for "Thirsty Thursdays" at a local club. While dancing, partying and hanging out with his ambitionless promiscuous party people and friends, Kermit quickly lost track of time and ended up waking up in a young lady's apartment the next day at 9:15 A.M., which means that Kermit was a full 1 hour and 15 minutes late to arrive for his shift and got to work still wearing the clothes from the night before. But clever Kermit sprayed on some cologne so that at least he smelled clean. You talked with Kermit 1 on 1 to make sure that he was okay, and yet he felt "singled out" and "like you are judging him" despite the fact that he had been to work on-time and consistently for the previous 3 weeks. Kermit, made the poor life choices, but Kermit is now mad at you yet again because you are the only person in his life attempting to hold him accountable.

FUN FACT

THE KERMITS OF THE WORLD HATE THIS VERSE.

"Lazy hands make for poverty, but diligent hands bring wealth."

- Proverbs 10:4

NOTABLE QUOTABLE

" Understand: people will constantly attack you in life. One of their main weapons will be to instill in you doubts about yourself – your worth, your abilities, your potential. They will often disguise this as their objective opinion, but invariably it has a political purpose – they want to keep you down."

- Robert Greene
(The best-selling author of *The 48 Laws of Power, Mastery, The 50th Law, The 33 Strategies of War,* and the *Laws of Human Nature,* etc.)

STEP 3

THE "YEAH BUT" PHASE

"YEAH BUT..."

-Bad Employees

It was on this day that Kermit began to passive aggressively disagree with you during a meeting for the first time.

During a meeting with your team you said, "It's super important that our website interface is easy to use for 99% of our customers." **And Kermit said,** "Well if our website doesn't provide extensive questions, badges and certificates of completion, then how can we really call ourselves the world's best?" **then you said,** "Kermit, we improved the lives of hundreds of our clients over the years." **In front of your whole team, the once coach-able, Kermit, now shouts,** "So, do you have a chart somewhere that could statistically prove that you know what you are talking about!?" **Kermit says this while being out of** dress-code, wearing skinny jeans, and sleeping with your former and still - married secretary, which are both violations your employee handbook.

Approximately 4 weeks ago, Kermit was appreciative, coach-able and committed to helping you achieve your goals. Now Kermit has become frustrated and has become a passive-aggressive member of the "I-Have-the-Courage-to-Bi%$*,-but-I-don't-have-the-courage-to-quit" club. Being a member of this exclusive club (known as 85% of the American population) allows Kermit to feel as though he has the upper hand and that you as the owner and founder should somehow feel bad because you don't agree with the consistently wrong world views, strategies and ideas of Kermit. This is where your employees start to attempt to take you hostage. He is now officially a part of the "I-am-too-valuable-to-fire" club so entitlement starts to set in.

STEP 4

THE "FOR THE GOOD OF THE BRAND" PHASE

At this point, Kermit is now going to openly disagree with you during a meeting where a large number of your teammates are present and he will start asking "Gotcha questions" during meetings.

At this point approximately 85% of employees (not everyone) are going to openly disagree with you during a meeting where a large number of your teammates are present and they are going to try to start asking "Gotcha questions" during meetings. As a hypothetical example, they will say, "I know that you say that social media is a waste of time 95% of the time, yet I saw you post..."

About 10 weeks ago, Kermit "was honored" to earn a job on your team and probably wrote some nice thank you notes about how you changed his life and he will never leave you because he is too grateful but now he has begun to openly disagree with you in front of your team, because Kermit is now "officially" on his way out. Now, he will never announce to you that he has fully committed to quitting because Kermit has now recognized the incredible super-move called, "The-Power-to-B$&%*,-While-Lacking-the-Power-to-Quit." **Kermit now looks unhappy most of the time while trying to play it off like a 4th grader that has just fallen off their skateboard.**

FUN FACT

The U.S. Chamber of Commerce estimates that 75% of employees steal from the workplace and that most do so repeatedly."

- CBS News

Employee Theft: Are You Blind to It?

NOTABLE QUOTABLE

" Every time I read a management or self-help book, I find myself saying, "That's fine, but that wasn't really the hard thing about the situation." The hard thing isn't setting a big, hairy, audacious goal. The hard thing is laying people off when you miss the big goal. The hard thing isn't hiring great people. The hard thing is when those "great people" develop a sense of entitlement and start demanding unreasonable things. The hard thing isn't setting up an organizational chart. The hard thing is getting people to communicate within the organization that you just designed. The hard thing isn't dreaming big. The hard thing is waking up in the middle of the night in a cold sweat when the dream turns into a nightmare."

- Ben Horowitz
(The best-selling author of *The Hard Thing About Hard Things* who sold his company Opsware to Hewlett-Packard for $1.6 billion in cash)

STEP 5

THE "OPENLY CHALLENGING" PHASE

The Kermits of the world are going to passionately refuse to follow your company's dress-code policy. By now you have found yourself by now saying things like, "Kermit, you know that I believe that we should always dress to impress and to over-dress to every business occasion, but you are not wearing a tie like everybody else. What's going on?"

"Well I just don't think that anybody is going to be interested in doing a business with a company where a bunch of dudes who are wearing suits." It started with a tie, then escalated to Kermit wearing jeans in the office, and eventually it resulted in Kermit wearing the same clothes from the day before because they started dating somebody at your office.

FUN FACT

"*78 percent of the men interviewed had cheated on their current partner.*"

- The Washington Post

5 Myths About Cheating

STEP 6

THE "P@$$IVE AGGRESSIVE" PHASE

They openly defy you by asking passive aggressive questions like,

"DO I REALLY NEED TO BE AT THIS MEETING? I DON'T KNOW WHETHER I AM REALLY ADDING VALUE TO THIS MEETING OR NOT? I'LL ATTEND, I MEAN IF YOU THINK THAT THIS MEETING ACTUALLY ADDS VALUE?"

They tried to trap you in yet another "gotcha question." If you require them to actually be at the mandatory meeting they will sulk and add no value, thus bringing the energy down in the meetings. Oftentimes, they will then openly attack anyone in the meeting that has tried to come up with a pragmatic and practical solution to a problem. They no longer ever come up with their own solutions. They just attack the others who do provide the solutions. If you told them "no," they would get their feelings hurt and they would still sulk. This is a lose-lose question and this is when the "not-showing-up-to-work" phase starts.

STEP 7

THE "CHECKED OUT" PHASE

COMMITMENT

THE ART

of the

No-Show

Passive aggressive people have the courage to quit working at their job emotionally, yet they lack the courage and the financial capacity needed to quit showing up to their job physically. These people start saying completely insincere statements like, "Can I just call in for today's meeting?" or "Do I really need to meet this week? We pretty much just go over the same stuff every week." And this is IF they actually decided to show up or call you at all. Their appearance becomes increasingly more and more rare. It is during this time of lamenting, venting, and secretly sharing their frustrations with everyone but you while they pursue a job at a company that directly competes with you. I've seen this process of becoming an anti-your-business-terrorist hundreds of times and what will happen next is never positive.

Put on a helmet, because you're about to be attacked.

FUN FACT

"*The unemployment rate has since crept up to 4% even though hiring remains quite strong.*"

- MarketWatch.com

Feb 7, 2019

NOTABLE QUOTABLE

"Only the paranoid survive."

- Andy Grove
(The former CEO and one of the
founding partners of Intel)

STEP 8

THE "PREPARE FOR WAR" PHASE

They now have become full-page, keyboard warriors who love to communicate exclusively via email.

The people who have decided to quit working with you, but who don't have the courage needed to actually quit getting paid by you love to communicate with you via email. Oh, yes! They do. In fact, they love writing this to you via e-mail and "certified mail" that they would never say to your face because they are too weak to be direct with you unless they are "high," "drunk" or they can use their wife or their attorney as a scapegoat with statements like, "hey, my wife just thinks I don't get paid what I'm worth" or "my attorney has advised me to do it this way." The types of emails that they send are always full of half-truths and content that is 99% emotional in nature. "I feel like you don't appreciate all that I have done for this company and for you," **and the** "I need to finally get paid what I'm worth. I've slaved away for you and I just can't believe I'm being treated like a dog!" **and things like that.**

They don't ever remember that you are the one that taught them everything they now know and that they are now using it to compete with you. When they send those types of emails, you can also guarantee that they will not be in the building later that week for you to discuss it in person.

When (if) they finally do show back up, they are all smiles and never, ever mention sending the email at all. This is assuming that they ever send you an email. Many times they will talk about you in a derogatory manner while hanging out with other employees or to their newest live in girlfriend when not writing false things about you on Reddit while courageously using an anonymous screen name. Before they leave, they want to create a weird atmosphere for both you and your current team.

STEP 9

THE "ALL OUT WAR" PHASE

At this point they have begun passive aggressively using slight legal threats like, "Well you will need to speak to my attorney," or "My uncle is an attorney and has advised me to speak to my attorney before communicating with you further." Once a chronic under-performer discovered that they are going to be fired from the job that they quit (mentally) showing up to (mentally) months ago, they then go out and hire a no-talent-ambulance-chasing attorney to represent them.

Once the Kermits of your life have moved on and have started something else, most of the time they will end up end up directly competing against you, and they will then create a business based on all of the things that you taught them. Their entitlement, bitterness, and feelings of being under-appreciated create a new monster called, "rage." They now begin using this rage in the form of suing you or invoicing you for work they did in the past that they "forgot to turn in." There is no win-win here. The damage is done and the relationship is irreparable. They will go around town dragging your name through the mud, so a super-move, is to call everyone that you both know first and let them know what actually happened. Warren Buffett said "It takes 20 years to build a reputation and five minutes to ruin it." So be sure to protect your reputation from lies and slander.

"Reputation is the cornerstone of power. Through reputation, alone you can intimidate and win: once you slip, however, you are vulnerable, and will be attacked on all sides. Make your reputation unassailable."

- Robert Greene
The 48 Laws of Power

NOTABLE QUOTABLE

"You have enemies? Good. That means you've stood up for something, sometime in your life."

- Winston Churchill

(The British politician, army officer, and writer. He was Prime Minister of the United Kingdom from 1940 to 1945, when he led Britain to victory in the Second World War, and again from 1951 to 1955.)

STEP 10

THE
"CAN'T MOVE ON"
PHASE

Since your ex-employee had no money, and they did not have any immediate success, they decided to invest their idle time (which is all of their time) suing you, booing you and writing bad online reviews about the success that you have built. Their bitterness is out of control here. They have decided to commit their days to sitting there and sulking while smoking pot. They only remember the times when you had to pull them aside and tell them to be on time, to get their job done, to hit deadlines, etc. They now resent you for ever having tried to help them become a better version of themselves. They hate you for your success and they want it for themselves but without making any sacrifices at all. Simply put, they loathed you, but lacked the courage needed to ever talk to you about it, or the brain to resolve it and move on. So, what did they do? They spent all of their free time (let's face it, there is a lot of it since they aren't employed) bashing you all over social media, suing you, and making up false stories of you. It is best to ignore them and let their burning passion for hating you flame out, much like their passion for working with you once did.

BIBLE VERSES

FOR KERMIT

PROVERBS 20:4

Sluggards do not plow in season; so at harvest time they look, but find nothing.

PROVERBS 6:9

How long will you lie there, you sluggard? When will you get up from your sleep?

PROVERBS 21:25

The craving of a sluggard will be the death of him, because his hands refuse to work.

CONCLUSION

The whole point of this book is to show you what can and will happen to you if you let employees and their problems fester. Between my partners and I, we've employed thousands of employees. I can honestly say that there are a few GREAT exceptions out there that do not fall into the 85% of employees category (in part, 15%). Today, I employ a great team of people who are here for a season to grow and are thankful for what they have learned. But there are also the terrorists employees that will try to hold you hostage. Do not let this be you. On the next pages, you'll see some action steps you can take to make sure you are never being held hostage.

1. NEVER S

"A SMALL TEAM OF A+ PLAYERS CAN RUN CIRCLES AROUND A GIANT TEAM OF B AND C PLAYERS."

– STEVE JOBS
(THE CO-FOUNDER OF APPLE, THE FORMER CEO OF PIXAR AND THE FOUNDER OF NEXT!)

OP HIRING

Even when you are fully staffed, never ever stop looking for great employees to make room for. Constant recruitment allows you to never be put into a bind or an awkward situation if an employee decides to move on.

2. NEVER ... GROUP I

"SOME PEOPLE AREN'T USED TO AN ENVIRONMENT WHERE EXCELLENCE IS EXPECTED."

— STEVE JOBS
(THE MAN WHO REVOLUTIONIZED THE COMPUTER, THE MUSIC, AND THE ANIMATED FILM INDUSTRIES)

TOP THE INTERVIEW

The group interview is a system I've refined over the past twenty years of self-employment where you can interview multiple people at the same time for the same position. This is powerful because it allows you to find/look for good people for an hour a week instead of having to allocate hours and hours a week to sit down and interview each person one-on-one.

3. NEVER ST
PEOPLE SI

"THE OLDER I GET THE LESS
I PAY ATTENTION TO WHAT
PEOPLE SAY AND THE MORE I
LOOK AT WHAT THEY DO."

— ANDREW CARNEGIE
(THE MAN WHO BECAME ONE OF THE WORLD'S
WEALTHIEST MEN IN HIS LIFETIME)

P HAVING
ADOW YOU

After you find a seemingly good person from the group interview, then have them shadow you for a day for the following reasons:

1. *Anyone can pretend to be awesome for an hour, but holding up the facade for several hours is a little bit more tough.*

2. *This is their opportunity to see what it is you do, and for you to build a foundation of your relationship with them.*

3. *This is your opportunity to see how they think and what level of skill they have for the job you are hiring them for.*

4. NEVER PUS
PAST THEIR

AN EMPLOYEE "LID"

The leadership expert John Maxwell talks about how each person has their own "lid," or their limit of competence. Once you try to push someone to be greater than they want to be, they will resent you for it.

5. NEVER TEAC
THE ENTIRE

AN EMPLOYEE USINESS

Each employee can have specific roles within the company, but once you teach an employee all of the ins-and-outs of the business, you have just created your future competitor.

6. MENTALL
UNCOACH

FIRE
BLE PEOPLE

When you watch an employee go from being coach-able and eager to learn, to being not open to feedback at all, mentally fire the person and replace them at the most convenient time for you, the business owner.

A BUSINESS EXISTS TO PLEASE THE OWNER.

- Dr. Robert Zoellner

Doctor Robert H. Zoellner has been a successful optometrist and entrepreneur within the city of Tulsa for over 22 years. However, most would consider him to be an entrepreneur first and an optometrist 2nd, 3rd, 4th, or 5th. As a self-made entrepreneur who started with nothing but passion, his current business ventures include: Z66 Auto Auction, Rockin' Z Ranch, Dr. ZZZ's Sleep Center, Dr. Robert H. Zoellner & Associates, and Thrive15.com.

He served as the Director of the Board for Regent Bank from March 2008 through January 2013. He's known for consistently saying, "I'd rather invest in a business I have control over." He has made enough money that he is now in that, "I'm going to wear a soccer jersey and shorts everywhere" phase of his life. He deeply cares about humans and is involved in countless philanthropic causes, not the least of which includes his benevolent tasering of Thrive15 Founder, Clay Clark.